Selection for One Piano, 4-Hands

from

MY FAIR LADY

Music by
FREDERICK LOEWE

Lyrics by
ALAN JAY LERNER

Arranged by Fr

Contents

chappell/intersong
music group—usa

EXCLUSIVELY DISTRIBUTED BY

HAL•LEONARD®
CORPORATION

7777 W. BLUEMOUND RD. P.O. BOX 13819 MILWAUKEE, WI 53213

Get Me To The Church On Time

Music by
FREDERICK LOEWE

Lyrics by
ALAN JAY LERNER
(*Lyrics not included*)

Allegro commodo

Secondo

Get Me To The Church On Time

Music by
FREDERICK LOEWE

Lyrics by
ALAN JAY LERNER
(*Lyrics not included*)

8

On The Street Where You Live

Music by
FREDERICK LOEWE

Lyrics by
ALAN JAY LERNER
(Lyrics not included)

On The Street Where You Live

Music by
FREDERICK LOEWE

Lyrics by
ALAN JAY LERNER
(Lyrics not included)

The Rain In Spain

Music by
FREDERICK LOEWE

Lyrics by
ALAN JAY LERNER
(Lyrics not included)

Tempo di habanera

The Rain In Spain

Music by
FREDERICK LOEWE

Lyrics by
ALAN JAY LERNER
(Lyrics not included)

Secondo

I've Grown Accustomed To Her Face

Music by
FREDERICK LOEWE

Lyrics by
ALAN JAY LERNER
(Lyrics not included)

I've Grown Accustomed To Her Face

Music by
FREDERICK LOEWE

Lyrics by
ALAN JAY LERNER
(Lyrics not included)

Show Me

Music by
FREDERICK LOEWE

Lyrics by
ALAN JAY LERNER
(Lyrics not included)

Show Me

Music by
FREDERICK LOEWE

Lyrics by
ALAN JAY LERNER
(Lyrics not included)

Wouldn't It Be Loverly?

Music by
FREDERICK LOEWE

Lyrics by
ALAN JAY LERNER
(Lyrics not included)

Secondo

Wouldn't It Be Loverly?

Music by
FREDERICK LOEWE

Lyrics by
ALAN JAY LERNER
(Lyrics not included)

Secondo

With A Little Bit Of Luck

Music by
FREDERICK LOEWE
Moderato

Lyrics by
ALAN JAY LERNER
(Lyrics not included)

Secondo

With A Little Bit Of Luck

Music by
FREDERICK LOEWE
Moderato

Lyrics by
ALAN JAY LERNER
(Lyrics not included)

Secondo

Primo

I Could Have Danced All Night

Music by
FREDERICK LOEWE

Lyrics by
ALAN JAY LERNER
(Lyrics not included)

I Could Have Danced All Night

Music by
FRÉDERICK LOEWE

Lyrics by
ALAN JAY LERNER
(*Lyrics not included*)

Secondo